AWESOME SUPER SIMPLE
HABITAT PROJECTS

SUPER SIMPLE

GRASSLAND

PROJECTS

FUN & EASY ANIMAL ENVIRONMENT ACTIVITIES

CAROLYN BERNHARDT

CONSULTING EDITOR, DIANE CRAIG, M.A./READING SPECIALIST

Super Sandcastle

An Imprint of Abdo Publishing
abdopublishing.com

abdopublishing.com

Published by Abdo Publishing, a division of ABDO, PO Box 398166, Minneapolis, Minnesota 55439. Copyright © 2017 by Abdo Consulting Group, Inc. International copyrights reserved in all countries. No part of this book may be reproduced in any form without written permission from the publisher. Super SandCastle™ is a trademark and logo of Abdo Publishing.

Printed in the United States of America, North Mankato, Minnesota
102016
012017

THIS BOOK CONTAINS RECYCLED MATERIALS

Editor: Liz Salzmann
Content Developer: Nancy Tuminelly
Cover and Interior Design and Production: Mighty Media, Inc.
Photo Credits: Mighty Media, Inc.; Shutterstock

The following manufacturers/names appearing in this book are trademarks:
Craft Smart®, Crayola®, Elmer's® Glue-All®, Gold Medal®, Morton®, Pyrex®, Scotch®

Publisher's Cataloging-in-Publication Data

Names: Bernhardt, Carolyn, author.
Title: Super simple grassland projects: fun & easy animal environment activities /
    by Carolyn Bernhardt.
Other titles: Fun & easy animal environment activities | Fun and easy animal
    environment activities
Description: Minneapolis, MN : Abdo Publishing, 2017. | Series: Awesome super
    simple habitat projects
Identifiers: LCCN 2016944668 | ISBN 9781680784411 (lib. bdg.) |
    ISBN 9781680797947 (ebook)
Subjects: LCSH: Habitats--Juvenile literature. | Habitat (Ecology)--
    Juvenile literature. | Grassland ecology--Juvenile literature.
Classification: DDC 577.4--dc23
LC record available at http://lccn.loc.gov/2016944668

Super SandCastle™ books are created by a team of professional educators, reading specialists, and content developers around five essential components—phonemic awareness, phonics, vocabulary, text comprehension, and fluency—to assist young readers as they develop reading skills and strategies and increase their general knowledge. All books are written, reviewed, and leveled for guided reading, early reading intervention, and Accelerated Reader™ programs for use in shared, guided, and independent reading and writing activities to support a balanced approach to literacy instruction.

To Adult Helpers

The projects in this book are fun and simple. There are just a few things to remember to keep kids safe. Some projects require the use of sharp objects. Also, kids may be using messy materials such as glue or paint. Make sure they protect their clothes and work surfaces. Review the projects before starting, and be ready to assist when necessary.

CONTENTS

GRASSLANDS
AROUND THE GLOBE

Did you know that one-fourth of Earth's land is covered in grasslands? They can be found on every continent except Antarctica. Grasslands usually exist in the drier parts of a continent.

Grasslands have lots of names! In the United States they are called prairies. South Americans call them pampas. They are known as savannas in Africa. But what makes a grassland? A grassland is a wide-open area where grass is the most common plant.

UNITED STATES PRAIRIE

AFRICAN SAVANNA

GRASSLAND ANIMALS

Grasslands can be tropical or temperate. Tropical grasslands are near the equator. It is always hot there. Tropical grasslands have a dry season and a rainy season. The African savanna is a tropical grassland. Common animals there include elephants, lions, and giraffes.

Temperate grasslands exist farther from the equator. They are drier than tropical grasslands. They are hot in the summer and cold in the winter. The prairie in the United States is a temperate grassland. Bison, jackrabbits, snakes, and coyotes live on the prairie.

PRAIRIE

SAVANNA

FARMS AND
GRASSLANDS

Much of the United States' grasslands have been turned into farms. This is because prairie soil is great for growing crops such as corn and soybeans.

SOYBEAN FIELD

More grasslands are turned into farms each year. This is because farmers are looking for ways to grow more crops. But grasslands are an important **habitat** for animals. We humans need to be careful about how much land we use. We must protect grassland animals and their habitats.

EAR OF CORN

SET IT ABLAZE!

Did you know that grasslands need to be regularly burned in order to stay healthy? Burning a prairie or savanna clears away trees and plants that would take over the grassland. These plants grow from the top, so the fire kills their growth. But grass grows from the bottom. This allows it to survive fire. The grass doesn't die. It just starts its growing process over again!

HABITAT
FOOD CHAIN

Every natural **habitat** has a food chain. The food chain shows what each animal eats. When humans harm a habitat, they ruin the food chain's balance. This causes some animals to go hungry.

GRASSLAND FOOD CHAIN

A food chain has several levels. The animals in one level mostly eat the animals in the level below. But some animals can be on more than one level.

The bottom, or level 1, of a food chain is plants. They make their own food from sunlight, air, and water. Level 2 of a food chain is **herbivores**. Level 3 is **carnivores** that eat herbivores. Level 4 is the top of a food chain. This level is carnivores that eat other carnivores. These animals have few predators.

4

3

2

1

LEVEL 1

GRASSLAND PLANTS

asters, buffalo grass, clover, lemon grass, red oat grass, sagebrush, star grass, sunflowers

ANIMAL AMBASSADOR

Jack Hanna loves wild animals! He has brought many animals onto popular television shows. Hanna uses these opportunities to teach about the threats animals and their **habitats** face. Many of the animals he teaches about live in grasslands. Hanna shows people around the world how to share their surroundings with amazing animals!

LEVEL 2

GRASSLAND HERBIVORES

bison, grasshoppers, rabbits, squirrels, termites, zebras

LEVEL 3

GRASSLAND CARNIVORES

aardvarks, mongooses, prairie chickens, skunks, snakes

LEVEL 4

GRASSLAND CARNIVORES

bobcats, cheetahs, coyotes, foxes, hawks, hyenas, lions, rattlesnakes

MATERIALS

Here are some of the materials that you will need for the projects in this book.

AIR-DRY CLAY

ALUMINUM FOIL

ALUMINUM PAN

BLACK TISSUE PAPER

BOWL

BROWN PAPER BAG

CARDBOARD

CORKBOARD

COTTON BALLS

CRAFT FOAM

DOUBLE-SIDED TAPE

FELT

FLOUR

FOOD COLORING

GLUE

GOOGLY EYES

GRASS

PAINT

PAINTBRUSH

POM-POMS

PUSHPINS

SALT

SAND

SCISSORS

SHOE BOX

SMALL ROUND MAGNETS

SOIL

SPRAY BOTTLE

TOOTHPICK

YARN

PRAIRIE ANIMAL
BURROW

MATERIALS: paper towel tube, scissors, clear jar, cardboard, paint, paintbrush, 2 pom-poms (1 large & 1 small), felt, glue, googly eyes, black tissue paper

Grasslands spread out as far as the eye can see! They are large and flat. This makes it hard for large animals to hide from predators. But hiding is easy for smaller animals on the grassland. Animals such as prairie dogs and foxes **burrow** into the ground. Being underground also protects burrowing animals from wildfires.

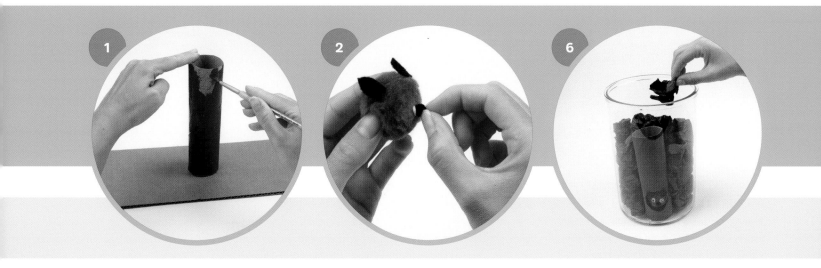

MAKE A COZY FOX DEN!

1 Cut the paper **towel** tube so it fits in the jar. Cut a hole near one end of the tube. Set the tube on a piece of cardboard. Paint the tube. Let it dry. This is the **burrow**.

2 Make a fox head. Cut ears out of felt. Glue the ears to a large pom-pom. Glue on a small pom-pom for the nose.

③ Glue on googly eyes. Let the glue dry.

④ Place the fox in the burrow. Make sure its face is in the hole. Glue the fox in place. Let the glue dry.

⑤ Put the burrow in the jar. Place it near the side so you can see the fox.

6 Crumple small pieces of black tissue paper. Put the tissue paper in the jar around the burrow.

BUSY WATERING HOLE

MATERIALS: aluminum pan, plastic cup, soil, jar lid, grass seed, spray bottle, plastic savanna animals, water, blue food dye

There is very little water on the African savanna during the dry season. The water is scattered in small watering holes. But the animals there are super smart! They always know how to find the watering holes. This means that watering holes are often packed with many animals!

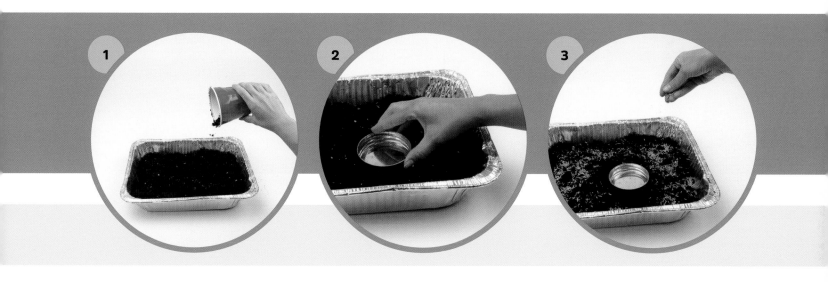

MAKE A MINI SAVANNA!

1 Fill the aluminum pan halfway with soil.

2 Place a jar lid in the soil. The rim of the lid should be level with the top of the soil. This is the watering hole.

3 Sprinkle grass seed over the soil. Add a little soil to cover the seeds.

4 Use a spray bottle to water the seeds. Place the pan in a sunny spot. Spray the seeds every day.

5 Once the grass starts growing, add savanna animals.

6 Put water in the jar lid. Add a drop of blue food coloring.

7 Watch your grassland grow wild!

HABITAT
SORT

MATERIALS: computer, printer, paper, scissors, word-processing program, glue, markers, craft foam, googly eyes, small round magnets

Grasslands exist in different parts of the world. Grasslands have different names, plants, and animals depending on where they are. Lions live on the African savanna. Coyotes live on prairies in North America. Horses and donkeys roam the steppes in Europe and Asia.

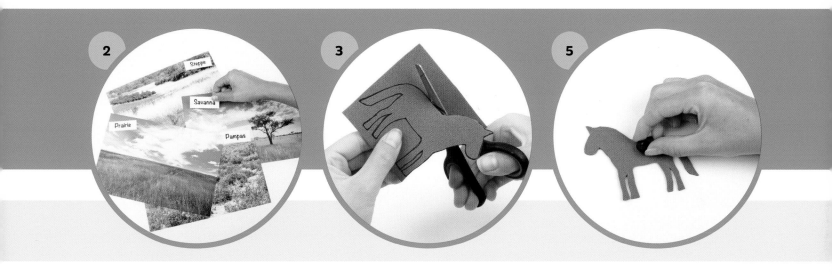

PLACE ANIMALS IN THEIR HABITATS!

① With adult help, **research** grasslands. Print out pictures of different grasslands.

② Type the grassland names in a word-processing program. Print them out. Cut the names apart to make labels.

Glue the labels to the correct pictures.

③ Draw animals from each grassland on craft foam. Cut out the animals.

④ Decorate the animals. Glue on googly eyes. Draw stripes, spots, and more.

⑤ Glue a magnet to the back of each animal. Let the glue dry.

⑥ Use the animal magnets to hang the grasslands on the refrigerator. Be sure to place each animal on the grassland where it lives.

SAVANNA
DIORAMA

MATERIALS: newspaper, shoe box, paint, paintbrush, scissors, cardboard, aluminum foil, cotton balls, glue, double-sided tape, grass, plastic cup, sand, brown paper bag, moss, air-dry clay, flowers, plastic savanna animals

African grasslands are famous! People often travel to the savanna to see the animals there. Lions, hyenas, giraffes, zebras, and elephants roam freely. When people visit the African savanna, it's called going on a safari.

GO ON A SAFARI!

① Cover your work surface with newspaper. Paint the inside of the shoe box blue. Let it dry.

② Cut a round piece of cardboard. Wrap foil around it. Paint the foil blue. Let it dry. This will be a watering hole.

③ Pull cotton balls apart. Glue them to the bottom of the box at one end. These are clouds.

④ Stick double-sided tape to the other end of the box. Stick blades of grass to the tape.

⑤ Tape the grass end of the box to the inside of the shoe box lid.

⑥ Put sand in the lid. Set the watering hole on the sand. Cover the edges of the watering hole with sand.

Continued on the next page.

SAVANNA DIORAMA (CONTINUED)

7 Cut a strip of paper bag and twist it. This will be a tree trunk.

8 Twist smaller strips for the branches. Tape the branches onto the trunk.

9 Glue moss to the tree branches. Let it dry.

10 Stick the bottom of the tree into a ball of air-dry clay.

11 Press the clay base of the tree onto the bottom of the box.

12 Place moss, grass, and flowers in the sand.

13 Set the animals on the sand. Imagine them roaming around on the real savanna!

DIGGING DEEPER

Many African animal populations are **declining**. This is partly due to **poaching** and **habitat** loss. But safaris are another reason for this decline. The areas where safari companies operate aren't always well taken care of. So, it can be hard for the animals to live there. The result is that many animals die.

One organization that watches animal populations is the International Union for Conservation of Nature (IUCN). It lists the **conservation status** of animals around the world.

CONSERVATION STATUS OF AFRICAN SAVANNA ANIMALS

CRITICALLY ENDANGERED
(EXTREMELY HIGH RISK OF EXTINCTION IN THE WILD)

BLACK RHINOCEROS

ENDANGERED
(HIGH RISK OF EXTINCTION IN THE WILD)

AFRICAN WILD DOG   PYGMY HIPPOPOTAMUS

VULNERABLE
(HIGH RISK OF ENDANGERMENT IN THE WILD)

HIPPOPOTAMUS   AFRICAN LION   CHEETAH   AFRICAN ELEPHANT

GRASSLAND
MAP

MATERIALS: computer, printer, scissors, marker, cardboard, measuring cups, ½ cup salt, 1 cup flour, bowl, spoon, ½ cup water, paper, glue, toothpick, newspaper, paint, paintbrush

There are grasslands all around the world! As you learned on page 4, every continent except Antarctica has grasslands. But each continent's grasslands are a little different.

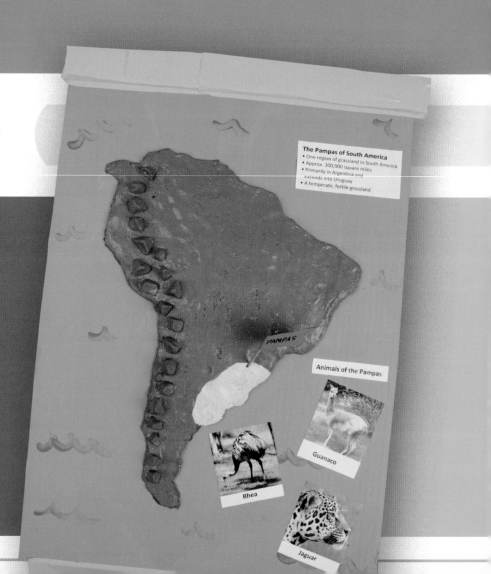

The Pampas of South America
- One region of grassland in South America
- Approx 300,000 square miles
- Primarily in Argentina and extends into Uruguay
- A temperate, fertile grassland

PAMPAS

Animals of the Pampas

Guanaco

Rhea

Jaguar

CREATE A CLAY CONTINENT!

① Have an adult help **research** the grasslands of the world. Choose the continent with grasslands that you like best.

② Print out a map of the continent. Cut it out.

③ Trace the continent onto the cardboard.

④ Put the salt and flour in the bowl. Stir them together.

⑤ Add the water a little at a time. Mix it in with your hands. The **dough** should stick together but not feel wet. If it gets too wet, add more flour.

⑥ Knead the dough until it is mixed well.

Continued on the next page.

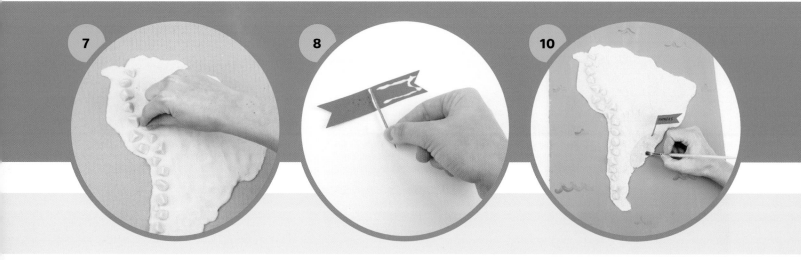

⑦ Press the **dough** onto the outline of the map. Add hills and mountains.

⑧ Cut a strip of paper. Fold it in half. Write the type of grassland on the paper. Glue it around a toothpick. Stick the toothpick in the map where the grassland is. Let the dough dry.

⑨ Cover your work surface with newspaper. Paint the cardboard blue. This is the ocean.

⑩ Paint the continent. Paint the grassland area a different color. Let the paint dry.

⑪ Make labels with facts about the grassland. Print and cut out pictures of animals that live there. Glue the pictures and labels to the cardboard.

DIGGING DEEPER

Why does the world have grasslands? Grasslands grow where there is not enough rain for a forest and too much rain for a desert. Some grasslands are bordered by mountains. The mountains block some of the rain so less falls on the grassland. This keeps it from turning into a full forest.

Today, some grasslands grow because animals **graze** on the plants and grass. This makes it hard for trees to take root. Wildfire is another cause of grasslands. The fire wipes out all plants to make way for grass! This is why controlled fire is an important part of keeping grasslands healthy.

MOUNTAINS BLOCKING RAIN

FIRE

GRAZING

FOOD CHAIN
CONNECTIONS

MATERIALS: computer, word-processing program, printer, paper, scissors, corkboard, double-sided tape, several colors of yarn, pushpins

On pages 8 and 9, you learned about the four levels of a food chain. These levels also have scientific names. Level 1 is producers. Level 2 is primary consumers. Level 3 is secondary consumers. Level 4 is **tertiary** consumers. Explore what each type of grassland consumer eats.

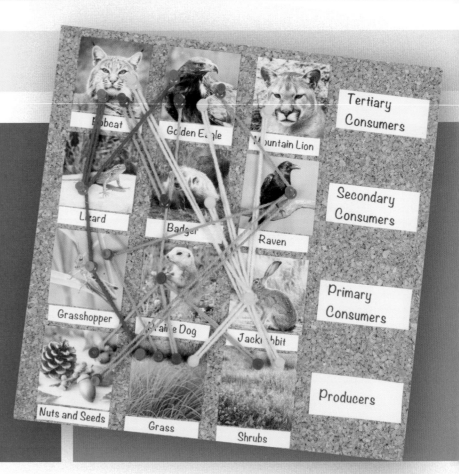

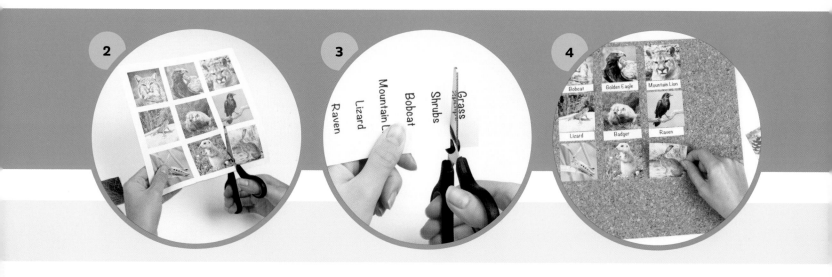

CREATE A WEB OF CONSUMERS!

1. With adult help, **research** grassland food chains. Find pictures of three **species** for each level.

2. Use a word-processing program to make the pictures the same size. Print the pictures. Cut them out.

3. Make labels for the species. Cut them out.

4. Arrange the pictures and labels on the corkboard. Put them in order with the **tertiary** consumers at the top. The producers should be at the bottom.

5. Use double-sided tape to stick the pictures and the labels to the corkboard.

Continued on the next page.

FOOD CHAIN CONNECTIONS (CONTINUED)

6 Make labels for the levels of the food chain. Tape them next to the correct levels.

7 Tie a piece of yarn to a pushpin. Stick the pin in one of the producers on the board.

8 Stick a pushpin in an animal that eats that producer. Wrap the yarn around the pin.

9 Stick a pushpin in an animal that eats the animal you marked in step 8. Wrap the yarn around the pin.

10 Continue adding pushpins and wrapping the yarn until you get to the top of the food chain.

11 Tie the yarn to the last pushpin. Cut off the extra yarn.

12 Repeat steps 7 through 10 to show other food chain connections.

DIGGING DEEPER

Food chains can be confusing! Animals can be on more than one level. For example, a bird is a primary consumer when it eats a plant. But when it eats a bug, the bird is a secondary consumer. When you put a lot of food chains together, they start to look like a spider's web! In fact, food chains are also called food webs.

Food webs are important! They tell us how sickness and pollution affect animals. For example, a certain **species** could get sick or die out. Then the animals that need that species for food will have less to eat. Those animals could die out too. Knowing what every animal eats helps us know how to protect animals and their **habitats**.

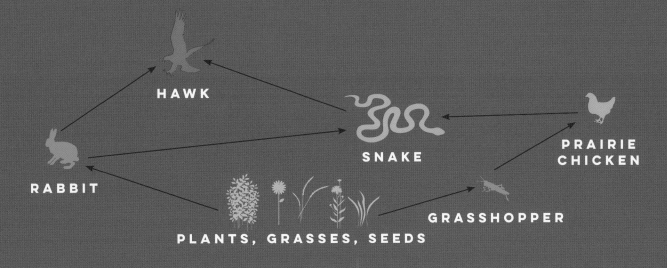

CONCLUSION

Grasslands are full of life! They support life for many different kinds of animals all across the globe. These animals have certain skills to live and flourish on a grassland. This book is the first step in learning more about grasslands. There is so much more to find out!

Do you live on or near a grassland? Have you ever visited one? Go to the library to **research** the world's grasslands. Or have an adult help you research grasslands **online**. Learn about what you can do to help preserve grasslands!

QUIZ

1 What continent doesn't have any grasslands?

2 What do small animals do to stay safe on the prairie?

3 Lions live in North America. TRUE OR FALSE?

THINK ABOUT IT!

What is your favorite grassland animal? Why do you like it?

Answers: 1. Antarctica   2. Burrow underground   3. False

GLOSSARY

burrow – 1. to dig a hole or tunnel in the ground to use for shelter. 2. a hole or tunnel in the ground that is used for shelter.

carnivore – an animal that eats mainly meat.

conservation status – a rating of how likely a species is to become endangered or extinct.

decline – to become less in number.

dough – a thick mixture of flour, water, and other ingredients.

graze – to eat growing grasses and plants.

habitat – the area or environment where a person or animal usually lives.

herbivore – an animal that eats mainly plants.

online – connected to the Internet.

poach – to hunt or fish illegally.

research – to find out more about something.

species – a group of related living beings.

tertiary – third in order, importance, or value.

towel – a cloth or paper used for cleaning or drying.